All about Edible Plants in Your Neighborhood

Children's Science & Nature

BABY PROFESSOR

EDUCATION KIDS

Speedy Publishing LLC
40 E. Main St. #1156
Newark, DE 19711
www.speedypublishing.com

Lots of people love gardening. Does your family have a garden of your own? A variety of plants may be grown indoors, and others outdoors... from pots to plots!

The vegetables on your dinner plate might just have come from your own backyard, and you didn't even realize they're edible!

Here are 15 healthy,
edible plants you
can help grow
right at home.

Avocado – Has healthy fats rich in vitamins A, E and B6. Eating these reduces the risk of cancer, heart disease, and eye degeneration.

Carrot – This is a good source of vitamins and minerals, including thiamin, niacin, folate, and potassium. Eating carrots boosts eye health.

Garlic greens –
A member of
the cancer-
fighting family.
These are the
greatest approved
superfood. Eating
them improves your
blood pressure,
lowers cholesterol,
and helps prevent
heart disease
and certain types
of cancer.

Lemon – This fruit is packed with vitamin C and antioxidants. This helps in decreasing the risk of heart disease and reduces inflammation. Lemon water gives you a boost to your immune system.

Mandarin Orange – Sweet tiny fruit which is another source of antioxidants. It also provides a good amount of calcium, magnesium, and fiber.

Microgreens – You might wonder what these are. These are seedlings of herbs and vegetables which might even have more nutrients than when they become adult plants. Eating a big bowl of these greens can be a stellar source of vitamins A, C, K, and folate.

Mushrooms – Edible mushrooms are fleshy and very flavorful. They're a great source of fiber and vitamin C. Antioxidants and cancer-fighting compounds are likewise present in them. Make sure you ask someone who knows about mushrooms which ones can be eaten safely!

Salad Greens –
The famous salad greens include iceberg lettuce, spinach, romaine lettuce, red leaf lettuce, and arugula. They are full of vitamins and minerals, including folate and iron.

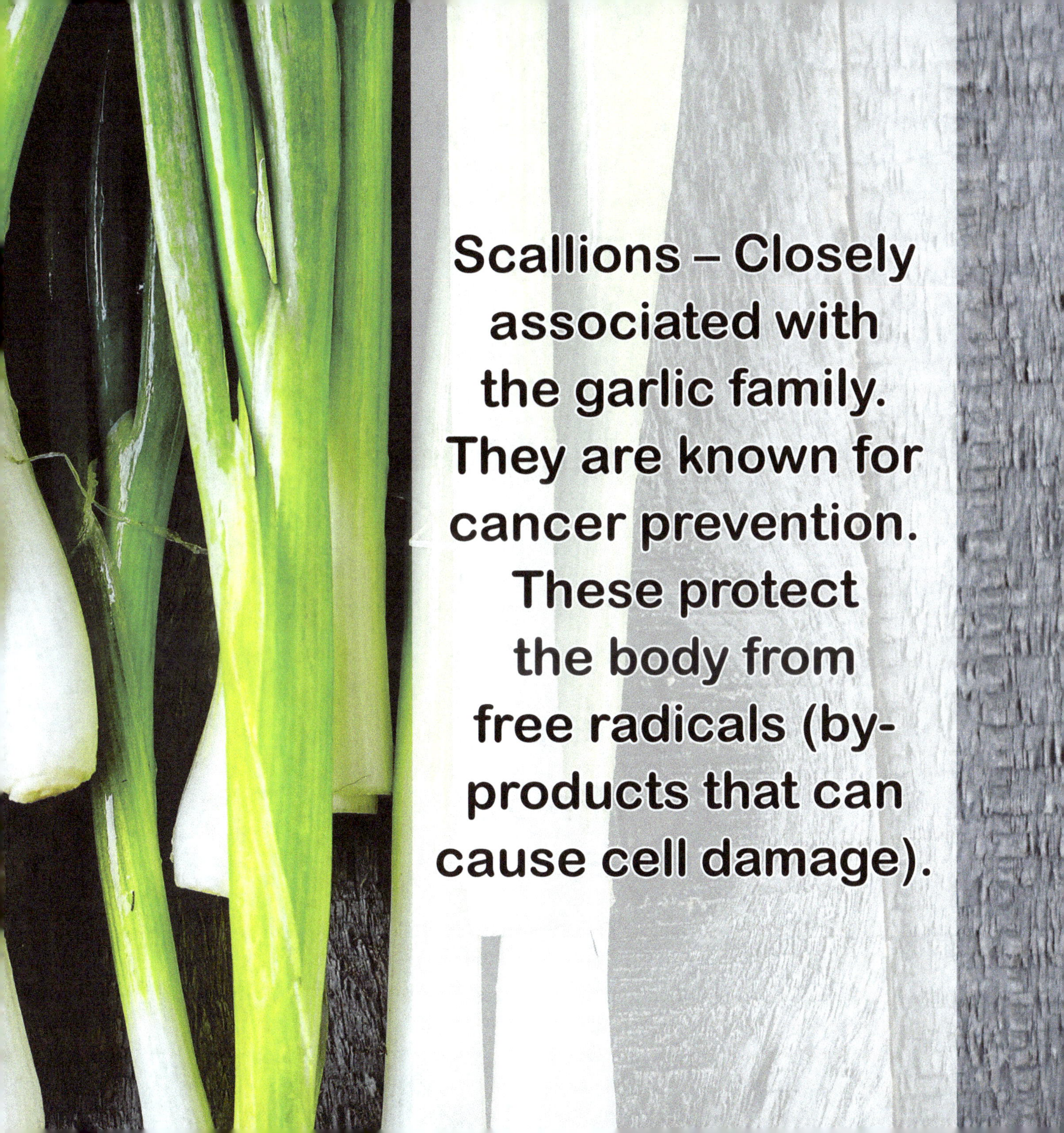

Scallions – Closely
associated with
the garlic family.
They are known for
cancer prevention.
These protect
the body from
free radicals (by-
products that can
cause cell damage).

Tomatoes – They are very rich in lycopene which has antioxidant and anti-inflammatory properties. These may help prevent coronary heart disease.

Basil – A very flavorful and aromatic herb that blocks enzymes in the body that causes swelling. Perfect for pasta dishes and veggie salads! Yum!

Chives –
Similarly, this herb is filled with antioxidants and phytochemicals. It is a known remedy that gives comfort whenever you have a stuffy nose or a cold.

Cilantro – These have highly concentrated amounts of carotenoids and are another good source of vitamin A. Cilantro can help prevent heart disease, stroke, and cancer. This herb is very low in calories and has zero cholesterol.

Ginger – This is a famous spicy superfood. This is known for its calming properties. If you get motion sickness and nausea, eat some ginger. It is also highly recommended for easing sore muscles, arthritis and even to slow the growth of cancer cells.

Mint – Tasty! But beyond that, this bright green herb actually aids digestion. It is a great appetizer and palate cleanser as it soothes and relieves the stomach.

These are your
most reliable and
healthy options
of free food right
within your reach.
Now you have
an idea what to
get and grow,
as these can
become staples
in your diet.

Visit
BABY PROFESSOR
EDUCATION KIDS
www.BabyProfessorBooks.com
to download Free Baby Professor eBooks
and view our catalog of new and exciting
Children's Books

www.ingramcontent.com/pod-product-compliance
Lightning Source LLC
Chambersburg PA
CBHW081241130726
47997CB00009B/2955